Edexcel GCSE (9–1)
Combined Science
Checklist 1

Contents

Published by Pearson Education Limited, 80 Strand, London WC2R 0RL.

Text © Mark Levesley, Penny Johnson, Sue Kearsey, Iain Brand, Nigel Saunders, Sue Robilliard, John Ling and Pearson Education Ltd.

Series editor: Mark Levesley

Typeset by Tech-Set Ltd, Gateshead.

Core design by Peter Stratton

The rights of Mark Levesley, Penny Johnson, Sue Kearsey, Iain Brand, Nigel Saunders, Sue Robilliard, and John Ling to be identified as authors of the work have been asserted by them in accordance with the Copyright, Designs and Patents Act 1988.

First published 2017

10 9 8 7 6 5 4 3 2 1

ISBN 9781292212951

Cover image: Fotolia/Vadimsadovski

Pearson

CB1a Microscopes

Step	Learning outcome	Had a look	Nearly there	Nailed it!
5th	Recall what an electron microscope is.	☐	☐	☐
5th	Recall what is meant by an instrument's resolution.	☐	☐	☐
5th	Explain why some cell structures can be seen with an electron microscope but not with a light microscope.	☐	☐	☐
7th	Calculate total magnification using an equation.	☐	☐	☐
7th	Calculate sizes using magnifications.	☐	☐	☐
5th	Interpret the SI prefixes milli-, micro-, nano- and pico-.	☐	☐	☐

CB1b Plant and animal cells

Step	Learning outcome	Had a look	Nearly there	Nailed it!
5th	Identify the parts of plant and animal cells.	☐	☐	☐
5th	Recall the parts of plant and animal cells.	☐	☐	☐
5th	Make drawings of plant and animal cells using a light microscope and identify their parts.	☐	☐	☐
6th	Describe the functions of the sub-cellular structures commonly found in eukaryotic cells (nucleus, cell membrane, cell wall, chloroplasts, mitochondria and ribosomes).	☐	☐	☐
6th	Estimate sizes using microscope fields of view.	☐	☐	☐
6th	Estimate sizes using scale bars.	☐	☐	☐

CB1c Specialised cells

Step	Learning outcome	Had a look	Nearly there	Nailed it!
6th	Describe how sperm cells are adapted to their function.	☐	☐	☐
6th	Describe how egg cells are adapted to their function.	☐	☐	☐
6th	Describe how ciliated epithelial cells are adapted to their function.	☐	☐	☐
7th	Draw conclusions about a cell's function from its adaptations.	☐	☐	☐

CB1d Inside bacteria

Step	Learning outcome	Had a look	Nearly there	Nailed it!
5th	Identify the common parts of bacteria.	☐	☐	☐
5th	Describe the functions of common parts of bacteria.	☐	☐	☐
6th	Describe why bacteria are classified as being prokaryotic.	☐	☐	☐
6th	Change numbers to and from standard form.	☐	☐	☐
8th	Compare eukaryotic and prokaryotic cells.	☐	☐	☐

CB1e Enzymes and nutrition

Step	Learning outcome	Had a look	Nearly there	Nailed it!
6th	State that enzymes are proteins.	☐	☐	☐
6th	Give examples of enzymes and where they are found in the human body and in other species.	☐	☐	☐
6th	Recall the subunits from which carbohydrates, proteins and lipids are formed (sugars, amino acids, fatty acids and glycerol).	☐	☐	☐
6th	Describe what enzymes do (catalyse the synthesis and breakdown of substances, such as carbohydrates, proteins and lipids, by speeding up the rate of reaction).	☐	☐	☐
6th	Describe an enzyme as a biological catalyst.	☐	☐	☐
7th	Explain why catalysis by enzymes is important for life processes (because reactions happen much faster).	☐	☐	☐

CB1f Enzyme action

Step	Learning outcome	Had a look	Nearly there	Nailed it!
7th	State the meaning of the term enzyme specificity.	☐	☐	☐
7th	State that an enzyme's action is due to its active site.	☐	☐	☐
7th	Describe the role of the active site in enzyme function (including specificity).	☐	☐	☐
9th	Use the lock-and-key model to develop explanations for enzyme activity.	☐	☐	☐
8th	Explain why enzymes have a particular shape, as a result of the sequence of amino acids in the chain.	☐	☐	☐
9th	Explain how enzymes become denatured.	☐	☐	☐

CB1g Enzyme activity

Step	Learning outcome	Had a look	Nearly there	Nailed it!
8th	Describe the effect of temperature on enzyme activity.	☐	☐	☐
8th	Describe the effect of substrate concentration on enzyme activity.	☐	☐	☐
8th	Describe the effect of pH on enzyme activity.	☐	☐	☐
8th	Explain what is meant by the optimum pH/temperature of an enzyme.	☐	☐	☐
9th	Calculate the rate of enzyme activity from experimental data.	☐	☐	☐
9th	Explain why temperature, substrate concentration and pH affect enzyme activity.	☐	☐	☐

CB1h Transporting substances

Step	Learning outcome	Had a look	Nearly there	Nailed it!
7th	State that substances are transported by diffusion, osmosis and active transport.	☐	☐	☐
7th	Describe how substances are transported by active transport (including the need for energy).	☐	☐	☐
6th	Explain how substances are transported by diffusion.	☐	☐	☐
9th	Explain how substances are transported by osmosis.	☐	☐	☐
9th	Explain the effects of osmosis on cells and tissues.	☐	☐	☐
8th	Investigate osmosis in potatoes.	☐	☐	☐
9th	Calculate percentage gain and loss of mass in osmosis.	☐	☐	☐

CB2a Mitosis

Step	Learning outcome	Had a look	Nearly there	Nailed it!
7th	List the names and order of the stages of the cell cycle, including mitosis.	☐	☐	☐
8th	Describe what happens in each stage of the cell cycle, including mitosis.	☐	☐	☐
7th	Describe why mitosis is important for an organism (growth, repair, asexual reproduction).	☐	☐	☐
9th	Explain why organisms may rely on asexual reproduction.	☐	☐	☐
7th	Describe how mitosis produces genetically identical, diploid cells.	☐	☐	☐
7th	Describe how cancers grow.	☐	☐	☐

CB2b Growth in animals

Step	Learning outcome	Had a look	Nearly there	Nailed it!
4th	Describe growth in animals as an increase in cell number and size.	☐	☐	☐
5th	Give examples of specialised animal cells.	☐	☐	☐
6th	Describe how structures of specialised animal cells are related to their functions.	☐	☐	☐
7th	Explain why cell differentiation is important in the development of specialised cells.	☐	☐	☐
8th	Use percentile growth curves to interpret growth in children.	☐	☐	☐

CB2c Growth in plants

Step	Learning outcome	Had a look	Nearly there	Nailed it!
8th	Describe the stages of growth in plants (cell division/mitosis, elongation, differentiation).	☐	☐	☐
5th	Give examples of specialised plant cells.	☐	☐	☐
6th	Describe how the structures of specialised plant cells are related to their functions.	☐	☐	☐
7th	Explain why cell differentiation is important in the development of specialised cells in plants.	☐	☐	☐

CB2d Stem cells

Step	Learning outcome	Had a look	Nearly there	Nailed it!
7th	Describe where stem cells are found.	☐	☐	☐
7th	Describe the function of stem cells in plants and animals.	☐	☐	☐
9th	Compare embryonic and adult stem cells in animals.	☐	☐	☐
7th	Give examples of where stem cells may be used in medicine.	☐	☐	☐
8th	Identify benefits and risks of using stem cells in medicine.	☐	☐	☐
10th	Evaluate the use of stem cells in medicine (by comparing their benefits and risks).	☐	☐	☐

CB2e The nervous system

Step	Learning outcome	Had a look	Nearly there	Nailed it!
6th	List the parts of the nervous system.	☐	☐	☐
4th	Describe how the nervous system detects stimuli.	☐	☐	☐
7th	Describe the structure of sensory neurones.	☐	☐	☐
7th	Describe the routes that impulses take to and from the brain.	☐	☐	☐
8th	Explain how sensory neurones are adapted to their functions (including the myelin sheath).	☐	☐	☐

CB2f Neurotransmission speeds

Step	Learning outcome	Had a look	Nearly there	Nailed it!
7th	Describe how the nervous system responds to stimuli.	☐	☐	☐
7th	Describe the structures of motor neurones and relay neurones.	☐	☐	☐
8th	Explain how motor neurones are adapted to their functions.	☐	☐	☐
9th	Explain the action and function of synapses.	☐	☐	☐
9th	Explain how the structure of the reflex arc allows a faster response.	☐	☐	☐
8th	Describe the structure and function of the reflex arc.	☐	☐	☐

CB3a Meiosis

Step	Learning outcome	Had a look	Nearly there	Nailed it!
7th	Recall that gametes are produced by meiosis.	☐	☐	☐
8th	Describe the overall outcome of meiosis.	☐	☐	☐
8th	Explain why haploid gametes are needed for sexual reproduction.	☐	☐	☐
6th	Recall what an organism's genome is.	☐	☐	☐
6th	Describe where genes are found.	☐	☐	☐
6th	Recall the function of genes.	☐	☐	☐

CB3b DNA

Step	Learning outcome	Had a look	Nearly there	Nailed it!
5th	Recall where DNA is found in a eukaryotic cell.	☐	☐	☐
7th	Name the bases in DNA.	☐	☐	☐
7th	Recall the pairing of bases in DNA.	☐	☐	☐
7th	Describe how DNA strands are held together.	☐	☐	☐
8th	Describe the overall structure of DNA.	☐	☐	☐
7th	Describe how DNA can be extracted from fruit.	☐	☐	☐

CB3c Alleles

Step	Learning outcome	Had a look	Nearly there	Nailed it!
6th	Describe the difference between a gene and an allele.	☐	☐	☐
8th	Explain the effects of alleles on inherited characteristics.	☐	☐	☐
7th	Describe the relationship between a genotype and a phenotype.	☐	☐	☐
7th	Identify homozygous and heterozygous genotypes.	☐	☐	☐
9th	Use genetic diagrams to work out possible combinations of alleles in the offspring of parents.	☐	☐	☐
9th	Explain why the effects of some alleles in an organism's genotype are not seen in its phenotype.	☐	☐	☐

CB3d Inheritance

Step	Learning outcome	Had a look	Nearly there	Nailed it!
8th	Use Punnett squares to work out possible combinations of alleles in the offspring of parents.	☐	☐	☐
9th	Interpret family pedigree charts to work out possible inherited genotypes and phenotypes.	☐	☐	☐
6th	Describe how sex is determined in humans.	☐	☐	☐
9th	Calculate ratios of phenotypes (controlled by alleles of a single gene) when organisms are crossed.	☐	☐	☐
9th	Calculate probabilities of certain phenotypes occurring when organisms are crossed.	☐	☐	☐

CB3e Gene mutation

Step	Learning outcome	Had a look	Nearly there	Nailed it!
6th	Give examples of characteristics controlled by multiple genes.	☐	☐	☐
6th	State the meaning of the term mutation.	☐	☐	☐
6th	Describe some potential applications of mapping human genomes.	☐	☐	☐
9th	Explain how a mutation can cause variation (limited to changes in the protein formed, which can affect processes in which that protein is needed).	☐	☐	☐
7th	Give examples of mutations in human genes that affect the phenotype, and examples of those that have little or no obvious effect.	☐	☐	☐
8th	Explain why many mutations have no effect on the phenotype.	☐	☐	☐

CB3f Variation

Step	Learning outcome	Had a look	Nearly there	Nailed it!
4th	Distinguish between genetic variation and environmental variation.	☐	☐	☐
5th	Distinguish between continuous and discontinuous variation.	☐	☐	☐
6th	Describe the causes of genetic variation (mutation and sexual reproduction).	☐	☐	☐
6th	Describe the causes of environmental variation (differences in the environment, acquired characteristics).	☐	☐	☐
7th	Analyse the contribution of genes and environment to the variation in a characteristic.	☐	☐	☐

CB4a Evidence for human evolution

Step	Learning outcome	Had a look	Nearly there	Nailed it!
4th	State the meaning of the term evolution.	☐	☐	☐
5th	Recognise binomial species names.	☐	☐	☐
7th	Explain how evidence from fossils and stone tools supports current ideas about human evolution.	☐	☐	☐
5th	Recall how stone tools are dated from their environments.	☐	☐	☐
6th	Describe how stone tools created by human-like species have developed over time.	☐	☐	☐
6th	Describe the fossil evidence for human-like species that lived 4.4, 3.2 and 1.6 million years ago.	☐	☐	☐

CB4b Darwin's theory

Step	Learning outcome	Had a look	Nearly there	Nailed it!
4th	Recall the cause of genetic variation.	☐	☐	☐
5th	Describe how adaptations allow organisms to survive.	☐	☐	☐
8th	Explain how natural selection allows some members of a species to survive better than others when conditions change.	☐	☐	☐
9th	Explain how natural selection can lead to the evolution of a new species.	☐	☐	☐
10th	Explain how the development of resistance in organisms supports Darwin's theory.	☐	☐	☐

CB4c Classification

Step	Learning outcome	Had a look	Nearly there	Nailed it!
5th	Describe how organisms are classified into smaller and smaller groups (based on their characteristics).	☐	☐	☐
6th	Identify genus and species from a binomial name.	☐	☐	☐
6th	Identify an organism as a member of one of the five kingdoms.	☐	☐	☐
7th	Describe what genetic analysis is.	☐	☐	☐
9th	Explain why biologists often now classify organisms into three domains.	☐	☐	☐

CB4d Breeds and varieties

Step	Learning outcome	Had a look	Nearly there	Nailed it!
7th	Describe why new breeds and varieties are created.	☐	☐	☐
7th	State the meaning of the term genetically modified organism.	☐	☐	☐
8th	Describe how selective breeding is carried out.	☐	☐	☐
10th	Explain the impact of selective breeding on domesticated plants and animals.	☐	☐	☐

CB4e Genes in agriculture and medicine

Step	Learning outcome	Had a look	Nearly there	Nailed it!
9th	H Describe the main stages of genetic engineering.	☐	☐	☐
7th	Recall some uses of selectively bred organisms (in agriculture).	☐	☐	☐
8th	Recall some uses of genetically engineered organisms (in agriculture, in medicine).	☐	☐	☐
11th	Evaluate the benefits and risks of using selective breeding and genetic engineering to produce new varieties and breeds.	☐	☐	☐

CB5a Health and disease

Step	Learning outcome	Had a look	Nearly there	Nailed it!
6th	State the meaning of the term health.	☐	☐	☐
5th	State the meaning of the term disease.	☐	☐	☐
6th	Describe how communicable and non-communicable diseases differ.	☐	☐	☐
7th	Outline the role of the immune system in protecting against disease.	☐	☐	☐
8th	Explain how disease can affect the immune system.	☐	☐	☐

CB5b Non-communicable diseases

Step	Learning outcome	Had a look	Nearly there	Nailed it!
5th	Give examples of non-communicable diseases.	☐	☐	☐
4th	State the meaning of the term malnutrition.	☐	☐	☐
5th	Explain how diet can lead to malnutrition.	☐	☐	☐
6th	Describe the link between alcohol and liver disease.	☐	☐	☐
7th	Explain the effect of alcohol consumption on liver disease at local, national and global levels.	☐	☐	☐

CB5c Cardiovascular disease

Step	Learning outcome	Had a look	Nearly there	Nailed it!
5th	Describe how obesity is measured (BMI and waist : hip calculations).	☐	☐	☐
6th	Describe how obesity correlates with cardiovascular disease.	☐	☐	☐
6th	Describe how smoking correlates with cardiovascular disease.	☐	☐	☐
6th	Explain why exercise and diet affect obesity.	☐	☐	☐
8th	Compare how cardiovascular diseases are treated	☐	☐	☐

CB5d Pathogens

Step	Learning outcome	Had a look	Nearly there	Nailed it!
5th	Describe some problems and diseases caused by bacteria.	☐	☐	☐
5th	Describe a disease caused by a virus.	☐	☐	☐
5th	Describe a disease caused by a protist	☐	☐	☐
5th	Describe a disease caused by a fungus.	☐	☐	☐
7th	Explain how signs of a disease can be used to identify the pathogen.	☐	☐	☐

CB5e Spreading pathogens

Step	Learning outcome	Had a look	Nearly there	Nailed it!
5th	State the ways in which pathogens can be spread.	☐	☐	☐
6th	Give examples of pathogens that are spread in different ways (e.g. cholera bacteria by water, tuberculosis bacteria and chalara dieback fungi by air, malaria protist by vector, *Helicobacter* by mouth, Ebola by body fluids).	☐	☐	☐
7th	Explain how the spread of different pathogens can be reduced or prevented.	☐	☐	☐

CB5f Physical and chemical barriers

Step	Learning outcome	Had a look	Nearly there	Nailed it!
8th	Explain how the spread of the STIs *Chlamydia* and HIV can be reduced or prevented.	☐	☐	☐
5th	Give examples of physical barriers.	☐	☐	☐
5th	Give examples of chemical barriers.	☐	☐	☐
6th	Describe how physical barriers protect the body (e.g. skin, mucus and cilia).	☐	☐	☐
6th	Describe how chemical barriers protect the body (e.g. lysozymes, hydrochloric acid).	☐	☐	☐

CB5g The immune system

Step	Learning outcome	Had a look	Nearly there	Nailed it!
5th	State that the immune system protects the body by attacking pathogens.	☐	☐	☐
7th	Describe how antigens trigger the release of antibodies and the production of memory lymphocytes.	☐	☐	☐
7th	Describe the role of antibodies in the immune response.	☐	☐	☐
7th	Describe the role of memory lymphocytes in triggering a secondary response.	☐	☐	☐
8th	Explain how immunisation protects against infection by a pathogen.	☐	☐	☐

CB5h Antibiotics

Step	Learning outcome	Had a look	Nearly there	Nailed it!
5th	Define the term antibiotic (as medicines that inhibit cell processes in bacteria).	☐	☐	☐
6th	Explain why antibiotics are useful for treating bacterial infections (because they do not damage human cell processes).	☐	☐	☐
6th	Explain why antibiotics cannot be used to treat infections by pathogens other than bacteria.	☐	☐	☐
6th	Describe the stages of development of new medicines.	☐	☐	☐
7th	Explain why each stage of the development of a new medicine is needed.	☐	☐	☐

CC1a States of matter

Step	Learning outcome	Had a look	Nearly there	Nailed it!
2nd	Name the three states of matter, and the physical changes that occur between them.	☐	☐	☐
5th	Describe the arrangements and movement of particles in the different states of matter.	☐	☐	☐
6th	Use information to predict the state of a substance.	☐	☐	☐
5th	Describe the relative energies of particles in the different states of matter.	☐	☐	☐
7th	Explain why the movement and arrangement of particles change during changes of state.	☐	☐	☐
7th	Explain why the energy of particles changes during changes of state.	☐	☐	☐

CC2 Methods of Separating and Purifying Substances

CC2a Mixtures

Step	Learning outcome	Had a look	Nearly there	Nailed it!
5th	Describe the differences between a pure substance and a mixture.	☐	☐	☐
5th	Use melting point information to decide whether a substance is pure or is a mixture.	☐	☐	☐
6th	Describe what happens to atoms at a pure substance's melting point.	☐	☐	☐
6th	Interpret a heating curve to identify a melting point.	☐	☐	☐
7th	Explain why the temperature does not change as a pure substance melts.	☐	☐	☐

CC2b Filtration and crystallisation

Step	Learning outcome	Had a look	Nearly there	Nailed it!
4th	State some mixtures that can be separated by filtration.	☐	☐	☐
4th	State some mixtures that can be separated by crystallisation.	☐	☐	☐
6th	Draw and interpret diagrams showing how filtration and crystallisation are done.	☐	☐	☐
6th	Explain the formation of crystals during crystallisation.	☐	☐	☐
5th	Explain how mixtures are separated by filtration.	☐	☐	☐
5th	Explain ways of reducing risk when separating mixtures by filtration and crystallisation.	☐	☐	☐

CC2c Paper chromatography

Step	Learning outcome	Had a look	Nearly there	Nailed it!
5th	Describe how some mixtures can be separated by chromatography.	☐	☐	☐
5th	Identify pure substances and mixtures on chromatograms.	☐	☐	☐
5th	Identify substances that are identical on chromatograms.	☐	☐	☐
6th	Draw and interpret diagrams showing how chromatography is done.	☐	☐	☐
6th	Explain how substances can be separated by chromatography.	☐	☐	☐
6th	Calculate R_f values and use them to identify substances.	☐	☐	☐

CC2d Distillation

Step	Learning outcome	Had a look	Nearly there	Nailed it!
5th	Describe how to carry out, and explain what happens in, simple distillation.	☐	☐	☐
7th	Distinguish between simple distillation and fractional distillation.	☐	☐	☐
7th	Identify when fractional distillation should be used to separate a mixture.	☐	☐	☐
7th	Describe how to carry out fractional distillation.	☐	☐	☐
9th	Explain how the products of fractional distillation are linked to the boiling points of the components.	☐	☐	☐
9th	Explain what precautions are needed to reduce risk in a distillation experiment.	☐	☐	☐

CC2e Drinking water

Step	Learning outcome	Had a look	Nearly there	Nailed it!
5th	Explain why water used in chemical analysis must not contain dissolved salts.	☐	☐	☐
5th	Describe how fresh water can be produced from seawater.	☐	☐	☐
5th	Describe the steps needed to make fresh water suitable for drinking.	☐	☐	☐
5th	Suggest how to purify water when you know what it contains.	☐	☐	☐
8th	Evaluate the hazards and control the risks present when purifying water.	☐	☐	☐

CC3a Structure of an atom

Step	Learning outcome	Had a look	Nearly there	Nailed it!
8th	Describe how Dalton's ideas about atoms have changed.	☐	☐	☐
8th	Describe how the subatomic particles are arranged in an atom.	☐	☐	☐
8th	Explain how atoms of different elements are different.	☐	☐	☐
7th	Recall the charges and relative masses of the three subatomic particles.	☐	☐	☐
8th	Explain why all atoms have no overall charge.	☐	☐	☐
8th	Describe how the size of an atom compares to the size of its nucleus.	☐	☐	☐

CC3b Atomic number and mass number

Step	Learning outcome	Had a look	Nearly there	Nailed it!
7th	State where most of the mass of an atom is found.	☐	☐	☐
7th	State the meaning of atomic number.	☐	☐	☐
7th	State the meaning of mass number.	☐	☐	☐
8th	Describe how the atoms of different elements vary.	☐	☐	☐
8th	State the number of electrons in an atom from its atomic number.	☐	☐	☐
8th	Calculate the numbers of protons, neutrons and electrons using atomic and mass numbers.	☐	☐	☐

CC3c Isotopes

Step	Learning outcome	Had a look	Nearly there	Nailed it!
7th	State the meaning of the term isotope.	☐	☐	☐
7th	Identify isotopes from information about the structure of atoms.	☐	☐	☐
8th	Calculate the numbers of protons, neutrons and electrons using atomic numbers and mass numbers.	☐	☐	☐
9th	Explain why the relative atomic mass of many elements is not a whole number.	☐	☐	☐
10th	H Calculate the relative atomic mass of an element from the relative masses and abundances of its isotopes.	☐	☐	☐

CC4a Elements and the periodic table

Step	Learning outcome	Had a look	Nearly there	Nailed it!
6th	Recall the chemical symbols of some common elements.	☐	☐	☐
6th	Describe how Mendeleev arranged elements into a periodic table.	☐	☐	☐
7th	Describe how Mendeleev predicted the existence and properties of some elements yet to be discovered.	☐	☐	☐
8th	Explain how Mendeleev's early ideas were supported by later evidence.	☐	☐	☐

CC4b Atomic number and the periodic table

Step	Learning outcome	Had a look	Nearly there	Nailed it!
7th	Explain some problems Mendeleev had when ordering the elements.	☐	☐	☐
6th	State the meaning of the term 'atomic number'.	☐	☐	☐
6th	Describe how the elements are arranged in the modern periodic table.	☐	☐	☐
6th	Recall the positions of metals and non-metals in the periodic table.	☐	☐	☐

CC4c Electronic configurations and the periodic table

Step	Learning outcome	Had a look	Nearly there	Nailed it!
6th	Recall the positions of metals and non-metals in the periodic table.	☐	☐	☐
7th	State the meaning of the term electronic configuration.	☐	☐	☐
8th	Show electronic configurations in the form 2.8.1 and as diagrams.	☐	☐	☐
9th	Predict the electronic configurations of the elements hydrogen to calcium.	☐	☐	☐
9th	Explain the links between an element's position in the periodic table and its electronic configuration.	☐	☐	☐

CC5a Ionic bonds

Step	Learning outcome	Had a look	Nearly there	Nailed it!
6th	Recall the formulae of simple ions.	☐	☐	☐
8th	Explain how cations and anions are formed.	☐	☐	☐
8th	Use dot and cross diagrams to explain how ionic bonds are formed.	☐	☐	☐
8th	Explain the difference between an atom and an ion.	☐	☐	☐
9th	Calculate the numbers of protons, neutrons and electrons in simple ions.	☐	☐	☐
9th	Explain the formation of ions in groups 1, 2, 6 and 7 of the periodic table.	☐	☐	☐

CC5b Ionic lattices

Step	Learning outcome	Had a look	Nearly there	Nailed it!
6th	Recall the formulae of common polyatomic ions, and the charges on them.	☐	☐	☐
7th	Interpret the use of –ide and –ate endings in the names of compounds.	☐	☐	☐
7th	Name ionic compounds using –ide and –ate endings.	☐	☐	☐
8th	Work out the formula of an ionic compound from the formulae of its ions.	☐	☐	☐
8th	Describe the structure of ionic compounds.	☐	☐	☐
8th	Explain how ionic compounds are held together.	☐	☐	☐

CC5c Properties of ionic compounds

Step	Learning outcome	Had a look	Nearly there	Nailed it!
5th	Describe the properties of ionic compounds.	☐	☐	☐
7th	Explain why ionic compounds have high melting points and high boiling points.	☐	☐	☐
7th	Explain why ionic compounds conduct electricity when they are molten and in aqueous solution.	☐	☐	☐
7th	Explain why ionic compounds do not conduct electricity as solids.	☐	☐	☐
7th	Identify ionic compounds from data about their properties.	☐	☐	☐

CC6a Covalent bonds

Step	Learning outcome	Had a look	Nearly there	Nailed it!
7th	Explain how covalent bonds are formed.	☐	☐	☐
5th	Recall the names of some common molecular elements.	☐	☐	☐
5th	Recall the names of some common molecular compounds.	☐	☐	☐
6th	State the bonding that is found in molecules.	☐	☐	☐
6th	State the approximate size (order or magnitude) of atoms and small molecules.	☐	☐	☐
8th	Explain the formation of covalent bonds using dot and cross diagrams.	☐	☐	☐

CC7a Molecular compounds

Step	Learning outcome	Had a look	Nearly there	Nailed it!
5th	Recall examples of common covalent, simple molecular compounds.	☐	☐	☐
6th	Describe the general properties of covalent, simple molecular compounds.	☐	☐	☐
8th	Explain why covalent, simple molecular compounds have low melting and boiling points.	☐	☐	☐
9th	Explain why covalent, simple molecular compounds are poor conductors of electricity.	☐	☐	☐
7th	Describe the structure of a polymer.	☐	☐	☐

CC7b Allotropes of carbon

Step	Learning outcome	Had a look	Nearly there	Nailed it!
5th	Recall some allotropes of carbon.	☐	☐	☐
7th	Describe the basic differences between covalent, simple molecules and giant covalent structures.	☐	☐	☐
7th	Describe the structures of diamond, graphite, fullerenes and graphene.	☐	☐	☐
6th	Describe the properties of diamond, graphite, fullerenes and graphene.	☐	☐	☐
9th	Explain the properties and uses of diamond and graphite in terms of their structure and bonding.	☐	☐	☐
9th	Explain the properties of fullerenes and graphene in terms of their structure and bonding.	☐	☐	☐

CC7c Properties of metals

Step	Learning outcome	Had a look	Nearly there	Nailed it!
6th	Describe the particles and how they are arranged in metals.	☐	☐	☐
7th	Explain why metals are malleable.	☐	☐	☐
7th	Explain why metals conduct electricity.	☐	☐	☐
3rd	Describe the typical properties of metals.	☐	☐	☐
3rd	Describe the typical properties of non-metals.	☐	☐	☐

CC7d Bonding metals

Step	Learning outcome	Had a look	Nearly there	Nailed it!
6th	Give examples of ionic; covalent, simple molecular; covalent, giant molecular; and metallic substances.	☐	☐	☐
7th	Describe how the different types of bonds and structures are formed.	☐	☐	☐
8th	Explain how the structure and bonding of a substance is linked to its physical properties. (Relative melting point and boiling point, relative solubility in water and ability to conduct electricity, as solids and in solution.)	☐	☐	☐
8th	Explain why we use models to represent structure and bonding.	☐	☐	☐
8th	Represent structures and bonding using a variety of different models (dot and cross, ball and stick, 2D, 3D).	☐	☐	☐
9th	Describe the limitations of the different models used to represent structure and bonding (dot and cross, ball and stick, 2D, 3D).	☐	☐	☐

CC8a Acids, alkalis and indicators

Step	Learning outcome	Had a look	Nearly there	Nailed it!
4th	Describe what the main hazard symbols mean.	☐	☐	☐
5th	Describe the safety precautions that should be observed when handling different acids and alkalis.	☐	☐	☐
4th	Name the ions present in all acidic and all alkaline solutions.	☐	☐	☐
5th	State the pH values associated with acidic, alkaline and neutral solutions.	☐	☐	☐
5th	Describe the effect of acids and alkalis on common indicators.	☐	☐	☐
5th	H Explain the link between pH and the concentration of ions in acids and alkalis.	☐	☐	☐

CC8b Looking at acids

Step	Learning outcome	Had a look	Nearly there	Nailed it!
5th	H Describe the relationship between hydrogen ion concentration and pH.	☐	☐	☐
5th	H Explain the difference between a dilute and concentrated solution (in terms of the amount of solute present).	☐	☐	☐
7th	H Explain the difference between strong and weak acids (in terms of the degree of dissociation of the acid molecules).	☐	☐	☐
7th	H Explain how the pH and reactivity of an acid depend on the concentration and the strength of the acid.	☐	☐	☐

CC8c Bases and salts

Step	Learning outcome	Had a look	Nearly there	Nailed it!
5th	Describe how a base reacts in a neutralisation reaction.	☐	☐	☐
6th	Describe what happens when an acid reacts with a metal oxide.	☐	☐	☐
7th	Write word equations for the reactions of acids and metal oxides.	☐	☐	☐
8th	Write symbol equations for the reactions of acids and metal oxides.	☐	☐	☐
6th	Explain what happens during a neutralisation reaction.	☐	☐	☐
6th	Describe the steps involved in preparing a soluble salt from an acid and an insoluble reactant.	☐	☐	☐
6th	Explain why: • an excess of insoluble reactant is used when preparing a soluble salt • the excess reactant is removed when preparing a soluble salt • the remaining solution contains only a salt and water, when preparing a soluble salt from an acid and an insoluble reactant.	☐	☐	☐

CC8d Alkalis and balancing equations

Step	Learning outcome	Had a look	Nearly there	Nailed it!
6th	Recall the chemical formulae of some common compounds.	☐	☐	☐
6th	Recall and use state symbols.	☐	☐	☐
9th	Balance chemical equations.	☐	☐	☐
4th	Recall that alkalis are soluble bases.	☐	☐	☐
6th	Describe the reactions of alkalis with acids.	☐	☐	☐

CC8e Alkalis and neutralisation

Step	Learning outcome	Had a look	Nearly there	Nailed it!
6th	Explain what happens to the ions from acids and alkalis during neutralisation.	☐	☐	☐
6th	Explain why titration is used to prepare soluble salts.	☐	☐	☐
6th	Describe how to carry out an acid–alkali titration.	☐	☐	☐

CC8f Reactions of acids with metals and carbonates

Step	Learning outcome	Had a look	Nearly there	Nailed it!
9th	H Write balanced ionic equations.	☐	☐	☐
7th	Explain the general reaction between an acid and a metal to produce a salt and hydrogen.	☐	☐	☐
7th	Explain the general reaction between an acid and a metal carbonate to produce a salt, water and carbon dioxide.	☐	☐	☐
5th	Describe the test for hydrogen.	☐	☐	☐
5th	Describe the test for carbon dioxide.	☐	☐	☐

CC8g Solubility

Step	Learning outcome	Had a look	Nearly there	Nailed it!
4th	Recall the general rules for the solubility of common substances in water.	☐	☐	☐
6th	Predict whether or not a precipitate will form from two solutions.	☐	☐	☐
6th	Name the precipitate formed in a reaction.	☐	☐	☐
6th	Describe how to prepare a pure, dry sample of an insoluble salt.	☐	☐	☐

CP1a Vectors and scalars

Step	Learning outcome	Had a look	Nearly there	Nailed it!
4th	Describe the difference between weight and mass.	☐	☐	☐
7th	Explain the difference between a vector and a scalar quantity.	☐	☐	☐
7th	Describe the difference between displacement and distance.	☐	☐	☐
7th	Describe the difference between velocity and speed.	☐	☐	☐
6th	State the meaning of the terms acceleration, force, momentum, energy.	☐	☐	☐

CP1b Distance/time graphs

Step	Learning outcome	Had a look	Nearly there	Nailed it!
7th	Recall and use equations relating distance, speed and time.	☐	☐	☐
6th	Interpret distance/time graphs (including recognising what the steepness of the line tells you).	☐	☐	☐
7th	Represent journeys on distance/time graphs.	☐	☐	☐
8th	Determine speed from the gradient of a distance/time graph.	☐	☐	☐
7th	Describe how speed can be measured in a school laboratory.	☐	☐	☐
5th	Recall typical speeds for walking, running, cycling and travelling by car.	☐	☐	☐

CP1c Acceleration

Step	Learning outcome	Had a look	Nearly there	Nailed it!
6th	Recall the equation relating acceleration, velocity and time.	☐	☐	☐
8th	Use the equation relating acceleration, velocity and time.	☐	☐	☐
6th	Recall the equation relating acceleration, velocity and distance.	☐	☐	☐
8th	Use the equation relating acceleration, velocity and distance.	☐	☐	☐
6th	Recall the acceleration in free fall.	☐	☐	☐
8th	Estimate the magnitudes of some everyday accelerations.	☐	☐	☐

CP1d Velocity/time graphs

Step	Learning outcome	Had a look	Nearly there	Nailed it!
7th	Represent journeys on velocity/time graphs.	☐	☐	☐
7th	Interpret velocity/time graphs qualitatively.	☐	☐	☐
8th	Calculate uniform accelerations from the gradients of velocity/time graphs.	☐	☐	☐
9th	Determine the distance travelled from the area under a velocity/time graph.	☐	☐	☐

CP2a Resultant forces

Step	Learning outcome	Had a look	Nearly there	Nailed it!
7th	Explain the difference between scalar and vector quantities.	☐	☐	☐
7th	Use arrows to represent the direction and magnitude of forces.	☐	☐	☐
6th	State the meaning of a resultant force.	☐	☐	☐
8th	Calculate resultant forces.	☐	☐	☐
6th	Explain whether forces on an object are balanced or unbalanced.	☐	☐	☐

CP2b Newton's First Law

Step	Learning outcome	Had a look	Nearly there	Nailed it!
5th	Describe the effect of balanced forces on moving and stationary objects.	☐	☐	☐
6th	Describe the effect of a non-zero resultant force on moving and stationary objects.	☐	☐	☐
7th	H Describe circular motion at constant speed as a changing velocity and hence as an acceleration.	☐	☐	☐
7th	H Describe the force needed to keep an object moving in a circular path.	☐	☐	☐
8th	H Give some examples of objects moving in circular paths and the type of centripetal force involved.	☐	☐	☐

CP2c Mass and weight

Step	Learning outcome	Had a look	Nearly there	Nailed it!
4th	Describe the difference between mass and weight.	☐	☐	☐
4th	List the factors that determine the weight of an object.	☐	☐	☐
4th	Recall the equation for calculating weight.	☐	☐	☐
7th	Use the equation relating weight, mass and gravitational field strength.	☐	☐	☐
4th	Describe how weight is measured.	☐	☐	☐
5th	Describe how the weight of an object is affected by gravitational field strength.	☐	☐	☐

CP2d Newton's Second Law

Step	Learning outcome	Had a look	Nearly there	Nailed it!
6th	Describe what an acceleration is.	☐	☐	☐
6th	List the factors that affect the acceleration of an object.	☐	☐	☐
6th	Recall the equation that relates the factors affecting acceleration.	☐	☐	☐
8th	Use the equation relating force, mass and acceleration.	☐	☐	☐
9th	Change the subject of the equation relating force, mass and acceleration.	☐	☐	☐
7th	H Explain what inertial mass means.	☐	☐	☐

CP2e Newton's Third Law

Step	Learning outcome	Had a look	Nearly there	Nailed it!
7th	Describe what Newton's Third Law says.	☐	☐	☐
7th	State the meaning of the term equilibrium situation.	☐	☐	☐
8th	Identify action–reaction pairs in familiar situations.	☐	☐	☐
8th	Distinguish between action–reaction pairs and balanced forces.	☐	☐	☐
8th	H Describe how objects affect each other when they collide.	☐	☐	☐

CP2f Momentum

Step	Learning outcome	Had a look	Nearly there	Nailed it!
7th	Describe the factors that affect the momentum of an object.	☐	☐	☐
9th	Calculate the momentum of moving objects.	☐	☐	☐
9th	Use the idea of conservation of momentum to calculate velocities of objects after collisions.	☐	☐	☐
8th	Describe examples of momentum in collisions.	☐	☐	☐
10th	Calculate the force needed to produce a change in momentum in a given time.	☐	☐	☐

CP2g Stopping distances

Step	Learning outcome	Had a look	Nearly there	Nailed it!
5th	Describe how human reaction times are measured.	☐	☐	☐
5th	Recall typical human reaction times and the factors that affect them.	☐	☐	☐
5th	Describe the link between stopping distance, thinking distance and braking distance.	☐	☐	☐
5th	Recall the factors that affect stopping distances.	☐	☐	☐
6th	Describe how different factors affect stopping distances.	☐	☐	☐
6th	Describe the factors that affect a driver's reaction time, including drugs and distractions.	☐	☐	☐

CP2h Crash hazards

Step	Learning outcome	Had a look	Nearly there	Nailed it!
10th	Calculate the force needed to produce a change in momentum in a given time.	☐	☐	☐
7th	Explain the meaning of the term large deceleration.	☐	☐	☐
6th	Describe the dangers caused by large decelerations.	☐	☐	☐
7th	Explain why large decelerations cause dangers.	☐	☐	☐
7th	H Recall some typical forces involved in road collisions.	☐	☐	☐
9th	H Use knowledge of changes in momentum to estimate the forces involved in road collisions.	☐	☐	☐

CP3 Conservation of Energy

CP3a Energy stores and transfers

Step	Learning outcome	Had a look	Nearly there	Nailed it!
6th	Interpret diagrams that represent energy transfers.	☐	☐	☐
7th	Represent energy transfers using diagrams.	☐	☐	☐
6th	Explain, using examples, that energy is conserved.	☐	☐	☐
5th	Give examples of energy being moved between different stores.	☐	☐	☐
7th	Describe what happens to wasted energy in energy transfers.	☐	☐	☐

CP3b Energy efficiency

Step	Learning outcome	Had a look	Nearly there	Nailed it!
8th	Explain some ways in which energy is transferred wastefully by mechanical processes.	☐	☐	☐
7th	Explain some ways of reducing unwanted energy transfers in mechanical processes.	☐	☐	☐
6th	State the meaning of the term efficiency.	☐	☐	☐
7th	H Explain how efficiency can be increased.	☐	☐	☐
9th	Recall and use the equation for calculating energy efficiency.	☐	☐	☐

CP3c Keeping warm

Step	Learning outcome	Had a look	Nearly there	Nailed it!
5th	Describe the ways in which energy can be transferred by heating.	☐	☐	☐
7th	Describe ways of reducing unwanted energy transfers using thermal insulation.	☐	☐	☐
5th	Explain how different ways of reducing energy transfer by heating work.	☐	☐	☐
5th	State the meaning of the term thermal conductivity.	☐	☐	☐
6th	Describe the effects of the thickness and thermal conductivity of the walls of a building on its rate of cooling.	☐	☐	☐

CP3d Stored energies

Step	Learning outcome	Had a look	Nearly there	Nailed it!
6th	Describe how different factors affect the gravitational potential energy stored in an object.	☐	☐	☐
8th	Recall and use the equation for gravitational potential energy.	☐	☐	☐
6th	Describe how different factors affect the kinetic energy stored in an object.	☐	☐	☐
8th	Recall and use the equation for kinetic energy.	☐	☐	☐

CP3e Non-renewable resources

Step	Learning outcome	Had a look	Nearly there	Nailed it!
4th	List the non-renewable energy resources in use today.	☐	☐	☐
5th	Describe the advantages and disadvantages of non-renewable energy resources.	☐	☐	☐
7th	Compare the advantages and disadvantages of non-renewable energy resources.	☐	☐	☐
6th	Explain how the use of non-renewable energy resources is changing.	☐	☐	☐

CP3f Renewable resources

Step	Learning outcome	Had a look	Nearly there	Nailed it!
4th	List the renewable energy resources in use today.	☐	☐	☐
5th	Describe the source of energy for different renewable resources.	☐	☐	☐
5th	Describe the ways in which the different energy resources are used.	☐	☐	☐
7th	Explain why we cannot use only renewable energy resources.	☐	☐	☐
6th	Explain how the use of renewable energy resources is changing.	☐	☐	☐

CP4a Describing waves

Step	Learning outcome	Had a look	Nearly there	Nailed it!
5th	Recall that waves transfer energy and information but do not transfer matter.	☐	☐	☐
5th	Describe waves using the terms frequency, wavelength, amplitude, period and velocity.	☐	☐	☐
6th	Describe the differences between longitudinal and transverse waves.	☐	☐	☐
4th	Give examples of transverse and longitudinal waves.	☐	☐	☐

CP4b Wave speeds

Step	Learning outcome	Had a look	Nearly there	Nailed it!
6th	Recall the equation relating wave speed, frequency and wavelength	☐	☐	☐
8th	Use the equation relating wave speed, frequency and wavelength.	☐	☐	☐
6th	Recall the equation relating wave speed, distance and time.	☐	☐	☐
8th	Use the equation relating wave speed, distance and time.	☐	☐	☐
7th	Describe how to measure the velocity of sound in air.	☐	☐	☐
7th	Describe how to measure the velocity of waves on the surface of water.	☐	☐	☐

CP4c Refraction

Step	Learning outcome	Had a look	Nearly there	Nailed it!
5th	Describe what refraction is.	☐	☐	☐
5th	Describe how the direction of a wave changes when it goes from one material to another.	☐	☐	☐
6th	Explain some effects of the refraction of light (explanations in terms of changing speeds are not expected).	☐	☐	☐
7th	H Explain how a change in wave speed can cause a change in direction.	☐	☐	☐

CP5a Electromagnetic waves

Step	Learning outcome	Had a look	Nearly there	Nailed it!
5th	Recall examples of electromagnetic waves.	☐	☐	☐
5th	Describe the common features of electromagnetic waves.	☐	☐	☐
5th	Describe the transfer of energy by electromagnetic waves.	☐	☐	☐
5th	Describe the range of electromagnetic waves that our eyes can detect.	☐	☐	☐
7th	H Describe an effect caused by the different velocities of electromagnetic waves in different substances.	☐	☐	☐

CP5b The electromagnetic spectrum

Step	Learning outcome	Had a look	Nearly there	Nailed it!
5th	Recall the groups of waves in the electromagnetic spectrum in order.	☐	☐	☐
5th	Recall the colours of the visible spectrum in order.	☐	☐	☐
5th	Describe how the waves in the electromagnetic spectrum are grouped.	☐	☐	☐
7th	H Describe some differences in the ways that different parts of the electromagnetic spectrum are absorbed and transmitted.	☐	☐	☐
8th	H Describe some differences in the ways that different parts of the electromagnetic spectrum are refracted and reflected.	☐	☐	☐

CP5c Using the long wavelengths

Step	Learning outcome	Had a look	Nearly there	Nailed it!
7th	H Describe how long wavelength electromagnetic waves are affected by different substances.	☐	☐	☐
7th	H Explain the effects caused by long wavelength electromagnetic waves travelling at different velocities in different substances.	☐	☐	☐
6th	Describe some uses of radio waves.	☐	☐	☐
6th	Describe some uses of microwaves.	☐	☐	☐
6th	Describe some uses of infrared.	☐	☐	☐
6th	Describe some uses of visible light.	☐	☐	☐
6th	H Describe how radio waves are produced and detected by electrical circuits.	☐	☐	☐

CP5d Using the short wavelengths

Step	Learning outcome	Had a look	Nearly there	Nailed it!
7th	⊞ Describe how short wavelength electromagnetic waves are affected by different substances.	☐	☐	☐
7th	⊞ Explain the effects caused by short wavelength electromagnetic waves travelling at different velocities in different substances.	☐	☐	☐
6th	Describe some uses of ultraviolet radiation.	☐	☐	☐
6th	Describe some uses of X-rays.	☐	☐	☐
6th	Describe some uses of gamma rays.	☐	☐	☐

CP5e EM radiation dangers

Step	Learning outcome	Had a look	Nearly there	Nailed it!
7th	Describe how the potential danger of electromagnetic radiation depends on its frequency.	☐	☐	☐
6th	Describe the harmful effects of microwave and infrared radiation.	☐	☐	☐
6th	Describe the harmful effects of ultraviolet radiation, X-rays and gamma rays.	☐	☐	☐
7th	Recall the nature of radiation produced by changes in atoms and their nuclei.	☐	☐	☐
7th	Recall that absorption of radiation can cause changes in atoms and their nuclei.	☐	☐	☐

CP6a Atomic models

Step	Learning outcome	Had a look	Nearly there	Nailed it!
7th	Describe the structure of an atom (in terms of nucleus and electrons).	☐	☐	☐
7th	State where most of the mass of an atom is found.	☐	☐	☐
7th	State the sizes of atoms and small molecules.	☐	☐	☐
8th	Describe an early model of the atom.	☐	☐	☐
8th	Describe how and why our model of the atom has changed over time, including the plum pudding model and the Rutherford alpha particle scattering experiment.	☐	☐	☐

CP6b Inside atoms

Step	Learning outcome	Had a look	Nearly there	Nailed it!
7th	State what is meant by an isotope.	☐	☐	☐
8th	Represent isotopes using symbols.	☐	☐	☐
8th	Explain how atoms of different elements are different (in terms of numbers of electrons and protons).	☐	☐	☐
7th	Recall the charges and relative masses of the three subatomic particles.	☐	☐	☐
8th	Explain why all atoms have no overall charge.	☐	☐	☐

CP6c Electrons and orbits

Step	Learning outcome	Had a look	Nearly there	Nailed it!
7th	Describe where electrons are found inside atoms (in terms of shells).	☐	☐	☐
8th	Describe when electrons can change orbit.	☐	☐	☐
7th	State the meaning of the term ion.	☐	☐	☐
8th	Describe how ionisation occurs.	☐	☐	☐
8th	Describe some of the evidence for the Bohr model of the atom.	☐	☐	☐

CP6d Background radiation

Step	Learning outcome	Had a look	Nearly there	Nailed it!
9th	Explain what background radiation is.	☐	☐	☐
9th	Describe how radiation measurements need to be corrected for background radiation.	☐	☐	☐
8th	List some sources of background radiation.	☐	☐	☐
8th	Describe how photographic film can be used to detect radioactivity.	☐	☐	☐
9th	Describe how a Geiger-Müller tube works.	☐	☐	☐
8th	Describe how the amount of radioactivity can be measured (in terms of the darkness of photographic film or by attaching a counter to a GM tube).	☐	☐	☐

CP6e Types of radiation

Step	Learning outcome	Had a look	Nearly there	Nailed it!
7th	Recall the relative masses and relative electric charges of protons, neutrons, electrons and positrons.	☐	☐	☐
8th	List five types of radiation that are emitted in random processes from unstable nuclei.	☐	☐	☐
8th	State which types of radiation are ionising radiations.	☐	☐	☐
8th	Describe what alpha and beta particles are.	☐	☐	☐
8th	Describe the nature of gamma radiation.	☐	☐	☐
11th	Compare the penetrating abilities of alpha, beta and gamma radiation.	☐	☐	☐
11th	Compare the ionisation abilities of alpha, beta and gamma radiation.	☐	☐	☐

CP6f Radioactive decay

Step	Learning outcome	Had a look	Nearly there	Nailed it!
9th	Describe the process of β⁻ decay.	☐	☐	☐
9th	Describe the process of β⁺ decay.	☐	☐	☐
10th	Explain how the proton and mass numbers are affected by different kinds of radioactive decay.	☐	☐	☐
9th	Describe what happens during nuclear rearrangement after radioactive decay.	☐	☐	☐
10th	Balance nuclear equations for mass and charge.	☐	☐	☐

CP6g Half-life

Step	Learning outcome	Had a look	Nearly there	Nailed it!
8th	Describe how the activity of a substance changes over time.	☐	☐	☐
8th	State how half-life can be used to describe the changing activity of a substance.	☐	☐	☐
8th	Recall the unit of activity.	☐	☐	☐
8th	Describe how half-life can be used to work out how much of a substance will decay in a certain time.	☐	☐	☐
10th	Carry out calculations involving half-life.	☐	☐	☐

CP6h Dangers of radioactivity

Step	Learning outcome	Had a look	Nearly there	Nailed it!
8th	Describe the hazards of ionising radiation in terms of tissue damage and possible mutations.	☐	☐	☐
9th	Explain the precautions taken to reduce the risks from radiation and ensure the safety of patients exposed to radiation.	☐	☐	☐
9th	Explain the precautions taken to reduce the risks from radiation and protect people who work with radiation.	☐	☐	☐
9th	Describe the differences between contamination and irradiation effects.	☐	☐	☐
11th	Compare the hazards of contamination and irradiation.	☐	☐	☐